I Choose

By: Suzin Helen Carr

Illustrated by: Chandler J. Carr

Choose well.
Peace,
Suzin
Chandler

For peace and our uncountable blessings.

Published in the United States of America by Illuminated Publishing, LLC.

ISBN-13: 978-0-615-22551-7
ISBN-10: 0-615-22551-9

Second printing February 2009

I choose. I choose.

I choose. Which shoes?

I choose to be mad…

...or to cuddle.

I choose to see sun in a puddle.

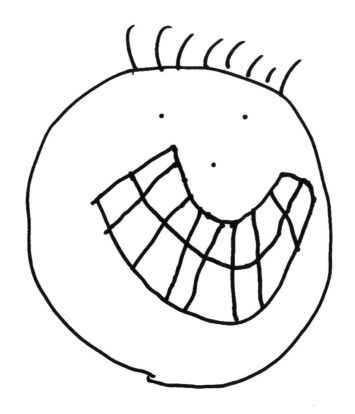

I choose to smile an inch or 4 feet.

I choose to be messy…

…or neat.

Whether I'm 6 or 60…it's the same.

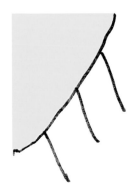

I choose how I finish a game.

I choose to be ups or be downs.

I choose between giggles and frowns.

I choose whether to hug…

…or to punch.

I know what is better for lunch.

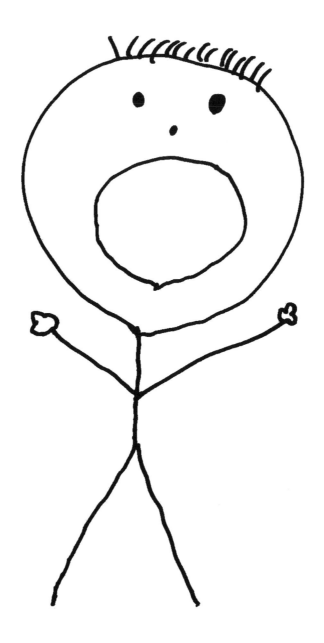

I choose whether to yell…

...or to sing.

I choose how much joy I will bring.

No matter what color my skin,

I choose the heart I live in.

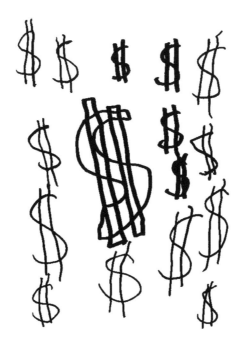

I may not be wealthy or poor,

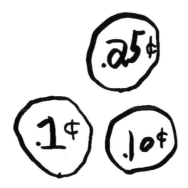

but I choose to be rich to the core.

I can't choose what lessons life brings,

I can choose what song my soul sings.

I choose to be the best I can be.

I choose…

...to be the me that is me!

Hooray!!!

Draw yourself as you choose…

Suzin H. Carr is the author of "I Choose", the wife of James, and the mother of Chandler. She lives in Lutz, Florida where she juggles the life she chooses and is grateful for countless blessings and immeasurable joy.

Chandler J. Carr was age 7 when he drew the artwork in this book. He plays wonderful guitar, loves video games and drawing and wants to be a video game designer when he grows up. He says that one of the most special things about him is his creative mind.